NORWAY

PHOTOGRAPHY BY ROBERT AND LOREN PAULSON

TEXT BY SIDNEY A. AND LOIS RAND

GRAPHIC ARTS CENTER PUBLISHING COMPANY, PORTLAND, OREGON

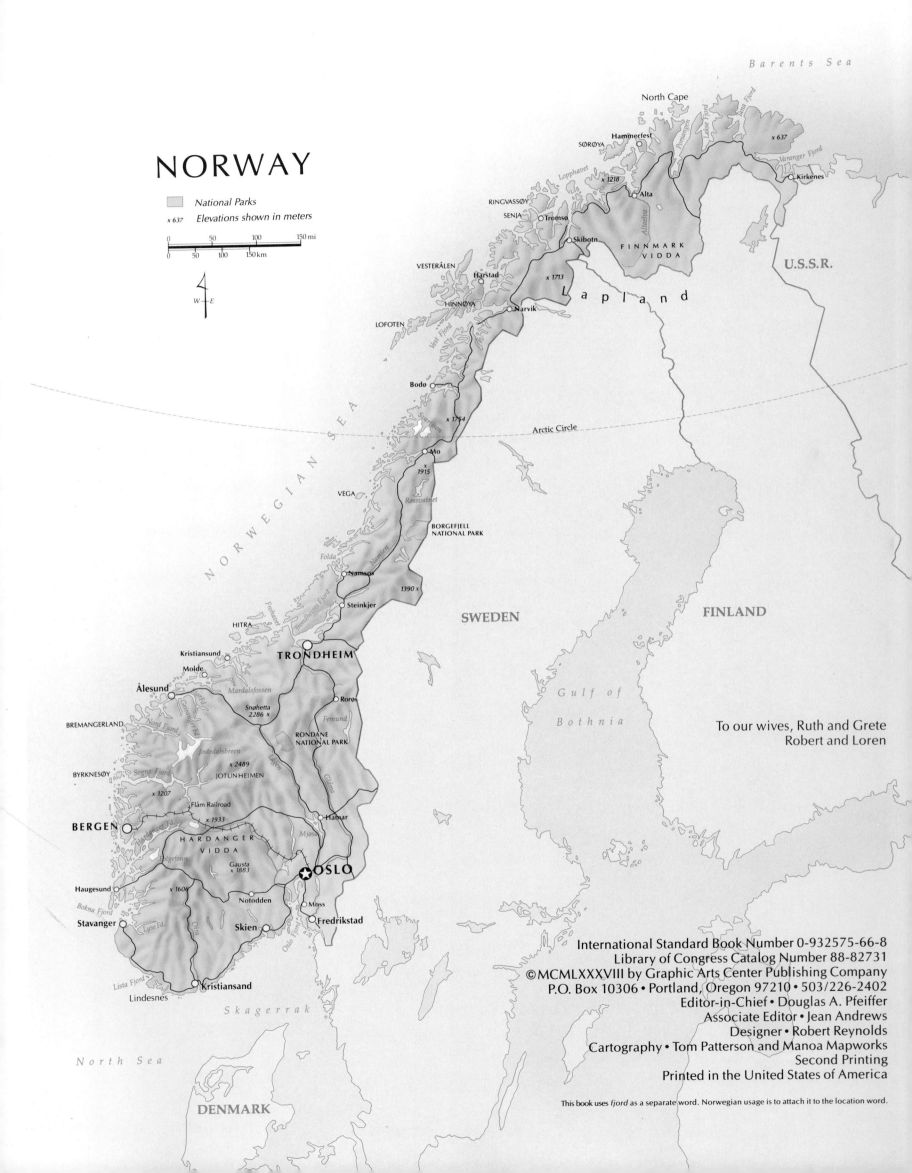

NORWAY

National Parks

x 637 Elevations shown in meters

50   100   150 mi
50   100   150 km

W — E

Barents Sea

North Cape
Hammerfest
SØRØYA
x 637
Varanger Fjord
Kirkenes
x 1218
Alta
RINGVASSØY
SENJA
Tromso
FINNMARK
VIDDA
Skibotn
VESTERÅLEN
Harstad
x 1713
L a p l a n d
HINNØYA
Narvik
LOFOTEN
Vest Fjord

U.S.S.R.

Bodø
x 1754
Arctic Circle
Svartisen
Mo
x 1915
VEGA
Rossvatnet
BORGEFJELL
NATIONAL PARK
Folda
Namsen
Namsos
1390 x
Steinkjer

SWEDEN

FINLAND

N O R W E G I A N   S E A

HITRA
Kristiansund
Molde
Ålesund
Mardalsfossen
Trondheims Fjord
TRONDHEIM
Roros
Snøhetta
2286 x
Femund
RONDANE
NATIONAL PARK
BREMANGERLAND
Nord Fjord
Jostedalsbreen
x 2489
JOTUNHEIMEN
*Gulf of
Bothnia*

To our wives, Ruth and Grete
Robert and Loren

BYRKNESØY
Sogne Fjord
x 1207
Flåm Railroad
x 1933
Gjende
Lågen
Glåma
Hamar
BERGEN
HARDANGER
VIDDA
Folgefonn
Gausta
x 1883
Mjøsa
OSLO
Hardanger Fd.
Sørfjorden
Haugesund
x 1606
Notodden
Moss
Bokna Fjord
Lyse Fd.
Otra
Skien
Fredrikstad
Oslo Fjord
Stavanger
Lista Fjord
Kristiansand
Lindesnes

S k a g e r r a k

North Sea

DENMARK

International Standard Book Number 0-932575-66-8
Library of Congress Catalog Number 88-82731
©MCMLXXXVIII by Graphic Arts Center Publishing Company
P.O. Box 10306 • Portland, Oregon 97210 • 503/226-2402
Editor-in-Chief • Douglas A. Pfeiffer
Associate Editor • Jean Andrews
Designer • Robert Reynolds
Cartography • Tom Patterson and Manoa Mapworks
Second Printing
Printed in the United States of America

This book uses *fjord* as a separate word. Norwegian usage is to attach it to the location word.

In a land of long winters, flowers are cherished. Among them is the oxeye daisy, called *prestekrage* or "pastor's collar" for the ruffled white collar worn by traditional clergy. Porsgrund, Norway's distinguished china manufacturer, salutes mountain wild flowers with a series of coffee-and-dessert place settings, each featuring a different variety painted by botanical artist Dagne Tande Lid.

Nidaros Cathedral in Trondheim, dating from the fourteenth century, is the largest church building in Scandinavia. Seven kings and three queens have been crowned here, the last being King Haakon VII who became king in 1905. A decision of Parliament altered the tradition, so when Olav V succeeded his father in 1957, he was not crowned, but was blessed in a religious ceremony.

Along Norway's west coast are magnificent fjords — narrow, glacially-formed arms of the sea reaching many miles inland. South of Ålesund, ships often sail into the Stor Fjord and maneuver their way between the cliffs of its remotest inlet, the Geiranger Fjord. Here, a small vessel sails past the fabled waterfalls, The Seven Sisters, toward the tiny village of Geiranger lying sheltered at the fjord's inner end.

■ *Above:* Pussy willows are a fresh touch of spring. ■ *Right:* Only 3 percent of the land is arable, and most farms are only a few acres tucked into valleys and hillsides. Farmers may raise wheat, oats, barley or potatoes, as well as keep a few dairy cattle, sheep, or goats. A farmer and his daughter at Folven in west Norway remove hay from the *hesje*, or hay fence, where it has been dried as fodder for the animals.

Cod hang in a fish-drying shed near Ålesund on one of 150 thousand islands along Norway's coast. Although fish is a popular part of the diet in Norway, 90 percent of the catch (mostly cod, capelin, herring, mackerel, salmon, and trout) is exported. Years of fishing experience have produced a subspecialty: a firm near Lake Mjøsa is the world's largest fishhook producer, distributing its products to 130 countries.

Near Fiskebøl in the Lofotens, a torrent of clear water rushes from its source in the snows of the mountains to its destiny in the Norwegian Sea. Although mountains here—with elevations in the three-thousand-foot range — are not as high as those farther south, the rough, barren beauty creates its own brand of enchantment. Those who live on these islands and fish the northern waters develop a rugged independence.

Lying at the south edge of a mighty glacier field, Bøyabreen, one of Norway's seventeen hundred glaciers, seems to meet the sky above and the settlement below. Its hovering presence, though spectacularly beautiful, is also useful. Glaciers cover 1.5 percent of Norway's land surface and provide water in abundance for many communities. They also offer some of the country's best ski terrain.

The glow of sunset lingering over fjord and mountains creates an ethereal scene on the west coast. Such vistas have earned Norway a worldwide reputation as a tourist attraction, yet it is also both a modern industrial nation and a social democracy committed to international peace and cooperation. The first Secretary General of the United Nations, Trygve Lie, was a Norwegian.

Spread on the hillsides surrounding the harbor, Bergen was home to distinguished composer Edvard Grieg and violinist Ole Bull. Each year in late May, the city hosts the Bergen International Festival of music, drama, ballet, and folk arts, which attracts performers and audiences from all over the world. Here, where rainfall is frequent, it is said that any baby born in Bergen comes with an umbrella.

Buildings with flowers and even trees growing on old sod roofs are a common sight in the countryside. Heavy log construction provides support for the roof. This storehouse, called a *stabbur,* has done its work and now rests in the Meldal Folk Museum south of Trondheim. Yet thousands of similar structures are in use all over the country.

Traditionally, the girls of a farm family would take cattle, sheep, or goats to a highland pasture each summer. One of Ole Bull's most evocative compositions describes such a girl, homesick on a Sunday morning as she hears church bells in the valley. Such a place is Elveseter, in the uplands between Dovrefjell and Jotunheimen. Its name tells the story, for *elve* means river, and *seter* means highland pasture.

THE SEACOAST

He was an American, a world traveler. One summer he found himself in a European tour group with Norway on its itinerary. This was a country he had never visited and with which he had not even remote ties.

He rode the tour bus over the mountain highways and onto the ferries, hiked the trails, scouted cities and farms, and shot the tourist's rolls of film. When he returned home, he exclaimed, "I have never seen anything so beautiful. Norway should be made an international park!"

This small, out-of-the-way country on the northwest edge of Europe affects most of its visitors this way. Yet when one realizes its rather remote geographical position, it is hard to imagine a less likely place for an "international park." The latitude of Norway — between 58° and 72° north — is only slightly farther north than the latitude of Alaska.

Forming the western border of the Scandinavian Peninsula, Norway is shaped like a tadpole, with an oval body forming its southern part and a long tail extending to the north. The country is eleven hundred miles long, roughly the distance from New Orleans to Minneapolis. Its width ranges from four to two hundred seventy-five miles, with a land area similar to that of New Mexico. It stretches from the Skagerrak and the North Sea on the south and west, to the Norwegian Sea and the Barents Sea on the north. Much of its border is seacoast, with the most direct route around the coastline 2,125 miles. Actually, because of the extreme irregularities of the coastline, the real sea perimeter is more like thirteen thousand miles.

Those unfamiliar with Norway might expect it to be a bitter, unwelcoming land, positioned as it is with the Arctic Circle bisecting it almost in the middle. Yet geography also provides it with a moderating boon in the form of the Gulf Stream, which moves from the south coast of the United States across the North Atlantic, to bathe the Norwegian seacoast and keep its waters ice free the entire year. As a result, average temperatures throughout coastal Norway are milder than this latitude would suggest — with temperate winters, cool summers, and abundant rainfall much like America's Pacific Northwest and Canada's British Columbia. Inland, Norway has warmer summers, colder winters, and less rain — similar to the weather in America's Upper Midwest. Traditionally, Norwegians thought in terms of two seasons, summer and winter. Spring and fall are imported concepts, regarded as brief reminders that the next season, a longer one, is approaching.

The dominant influence on Norwegian life is the sea. It is therefore helpful to view the country first from the seacoast, a journey often made by travelers in search of natural splendor.

They are not disappointed, for in addition to the constant extremes of mountains and valleys, there are two dramatic features that distinguish this seacoast from nearly all others. These are the Skjærgard and the fjords.

The mainland is protected from the open ocean by a necklace of about one hundred fifty thousand islands called the Skjærgard, or "rock fence," representing a significant 7 percent of the total land area. They shelter old harbors, large and small, that for centuries have served an unending stream of seafarers who have demonstrated Norway's maritime prowess across the world's oceans.

Along the entire coastline are many fjords, those narrow fingers of the sea stretching inland, some for more than a hundred miles. They are sharply defined by steep cliffs rising from the water's edge and reaching down to ocean depths, which distinguish them from ordinary bays and inlets. Most of these one-time glacial valleys lie along the west coast, with the most dramatic of them in the southern third of the country.

Approaching Norway by boat across the Skagerrak from the continent, one sees jagged mainland border and coastal islands fringed with white frame dwellings and countless piers and boat docks. The sails of pleasure boats mingle with fishing and cargo vessels on blue waters along a shore mottled with small fields and wooded hills.

Kristiansand, a community of sixty-five thousand, is the best-known port on the south coast. Situated on a small peninsula, its central area is laid out in uniform, rectangular blocks, a highly unusual configuration in a country where people's living arrangements are almost totally at the mercy of an irregular terrain. Kristiansand has a long history as a commercial and shipping center, and remains the focal point for rail and auto traffic seeking south coast shipping facilities for timber, metallurgical, and agricultural products bound for other countries.

Sailing westward, one skirts a landscape filled with contrasts. At water's edge, well-cultivated fields thrive on moraine land, before a backdrop of rock or heather-clad hillsides. Near Stavanger, an important harbor since its founding in the eighth century, the true fjord country begins as the southwesterly curve of shoreline bends to the north. It has always been a key fishing port, and was the embarkation point in 1825 for the sloop, *Restaurationen*, which carried the first fifty-two emigrants leaving for the New World.

In the 1970s, after oil was discovered in the North Sea, Stavanger became a boom town of foreigners mingled with natives. The population now totals nearly one hundred thousand. As the first center for Norway's emerging petroleum industry, Stavanger found its historical emphasis on fishing and canneries nearly elbowed aside by rapid change. Today, the port is

Nearing the finish line

Fun on the Oslo Fjord

busy not only with boats, but with the construction of off-shore oil rigs. The town combines the old-world charm of narrow, winding streets and an eight-hundred-year-old cathedral alongside the construction projects and commercial bustle of the energy business.

North from Stavanger, the islands of the Skjærgard, some inhabited but many not, proliferate in number, and increase in cragginess and size. A boat can wend its way through their channels into the Hardanger Fjord via smaller fjords just north of Haugesund. The surrounding, heavily wooded mountains are often snow capped, occasionally reaching elevations of five thousand feet. Such elevations do not impress mountain lovers, that is, until they glimpse a peak rising directly from sea level, reflected in quiet, deep-blue fjord waters.

Undoubtedly the best-known western port is Bergen. With a population of 210,000, this is the second-largest city in Norway, next in size to Oslo, the capital. Centuries ago, Bergen was a commercial center linked with other countries, while Oslo was still a village. The land rises quickly to provide a sort of amphitheater around Bergen's excellent harbor. Ships docking there offer a close-up view of its famed Hanseatic wharf with its cluster of buildings dating from the Middle Ages, once the focal point of trade and cosmopolitan activity with Europe. Sharing the wharf with this bit of history is the equally well known open-air market, a daily delight for sightseers as well as shoppers for fish, meat, fruit, vegetables, and flowers.

At Bergen, as at all the major ports, the air is filled with the briny tang that surrounds fishing vessels returning from successful runs. Sea gulls swoop and shriek overhead. Cruise ships disgorge hundreds of passengers with cameras and hiking shoes, bound for a few hours of land pleasures. Freighters load cargo destined for faraway places. Amid these imposing ships maneuver hundreds of small craft engaged in more private forms of business or pleasure.

The rest of Bergen, strewn up the hillsides, is a business and cultural center, as well as the south entrance to the most popular tourist area of the country, which includes numerous fjords, mountains, and plateaus. A favorite trip for visitors is a ride on the funicular railway up to Fløyen Restaurant for a bird's-eye view of the harbor. Music lovers covet a concert at the magnificent concert house, Grieghallen, or at Troldhaugen, the home of Edvard Grieg. Each year in late May and early June, Bergen hosts an arts festival that attracts performing artists from all over the world.

North from Bergen, there is another, and very special, option for viewing the coast of Norway. One can book passage on the *Hurtigrute,* the "fast route," a fleet of daily service boats plying western and northern waters. Although it is a comparatively slow and leisurely route today, taking eleven days to make the round trip to Kirkenes and back, it deserved its name in the days when inland transportation to the northern reaches of Norway was next to impossible. *Hurtigrute* boats stop at thirty-five ports, delivering and taking on passengers, mail, and commercial cargo. In America, it would be called a milk run, yet each year twenty-one thousand tourists manage to take this trip along with the local travelers. The newest ship of the line has two hundred berths and space for forty cars.

The passenger sailing north from Bergen is invariably stunned by the prodigal beauty of islands, peninsulas, mountains, and villages mixed helter-skelter among bays, estuaries, straits, fjords, and silvery waterfalls. Nothing here is as tame as a cove! Trying to follow the coastline from Bergen to Trondheim on a map is thoroughly bewildering, yet around each curve is a splendor more dazzling than the last.

About sixty miles north of Bergen lies the Sogne Fjord, which runs inland for 125 miles and reaches a maximum depth of over four thousand feet. It and its slightly shorter, but more northerly, sisters — the Nord Fjord and the Stor Fjord — are featured destinations for travelers by cruise ship, train, boat, and auto. Visitors jostle for camera angles adequate to capture even a part of the stunning vistas to share with those back home.

Cruise ships come all the way inland on several of the fjords, including the Sogne Fjord, and a network of ferries runs regularly to accommodate land travelers, as well as local commuters crisscrossing the fjord country. In fact, on the Sogne Fjord, there is opportunity to change from an auto-bearing ferry to another in the middle of the fjord.

One of the cruise tourists' favorite side trips is to debark at Flåm at the inner end of Aurlands Fjord, an arm of the Sogne Fjord, and ride by electric train up three thousand feet on a twelve-mile trip to Myrdal. From there, one can take a tour bus to the spectacularly situated resort, Stalheim, then down a road of tight hairpin curves to rejoin the ship at Gudvangen on a nearby arm of the fjord.

Shorter in length than the Sogne Fjord, the Nord Fjord is no less lovely. In the nearby mountains lies Lake Horningdal — at 1,650 feet the deepest lake in Europe. Ages ago, it was an arm of the fjord; its waters still tumble and fall through crevices to join the sea waters of the fjord below.

Next comes the winding Stor Fjord, whose innermost arm is the fabled Geiranger Fjord. This last narrow channel has been pictured on more postcards than perhaps any other Norwegian scenery. Here are Bridal Veil Falls, Pulpit Rock, and the Seven Sisters Falls with their sheer, parallel drops of hundreds of feet. At the fjord's inner end is the tiny town of Geiranger, where one can debark for a side trip up to one of Norway's many glaciers.

Ferries for people and cars

At the mouth of the Stor Fjord lies Ålesund, a town built on three islands that enclose its harbor. Homes cling to hillsides and ribbons of shore, giving the city an almost mythical charm. Not surprisingly, it is as popular for vacationing as it is utilitarian for fishing and industrial shipping.

Trondheim, a city of 135,000, lies at the mouth of the river Nid in the sheltered Trondheims Fjord, where the meeting of sea and land is less violent. The port bustles with activity, as it has since the early Middle Ages when Trondheim flourished as an important trading center and fortress city. It was a focal point both for power struggles and for religious pilgrimages. Old buildings fringe the water and cluster around Nidaros Cathedral, the largest and most famous church in Norway. The fjord spreads out in a broad sweep from the harbor, and the hills here are more rolling than rugged.

Many people, both Norwegians and visitors, think of Trondheim as the "north end" of Norway. Yet beyond this port lies the longest part of the journey. Boats thread their way through swarms of islands, many with tiny plots of green and scatterings of homes in the most improbable places. Generally, the land becomes wilder, the rocks rougher, timberlines lower, and the soil less fertile. Occasionally an island juts abruptly skyward as if in surprise at its fairyland setting.

Soon after crossing the Arctic Circle, ships dock at Bodø, a town of only thirty-five thousand, which lays claim to being the oldest city in the region. It is the gateway to the real north, say the northerners, and is the last station on the Norway railway system. Beyond this point, the substratum is too weak to support a railway line.

Beyond Bodø, at much the same latitude as northern Alaska, the Skjærgard broadens as the continental shelf extends farther into the sea and forms two specific cluster of islands, the Lofotens and the Vesterålens. Both are characterized by steep, jagged peaks and the storms associated with the sea. Enormous colonies of sea birds create a sense of motion on the cliffs. Tiny fishing villages cling to low spits of land on what must certainly rank among the world's most spectacular home sites, inhabited, certainly, by some of the world's hardiest residents.

Having sailed the tricky course between the islands and the mainland, ships find harbor at Tromsø, which claims for itself the title, "Paris of the North"—a small Paris, indeed, at just fifty thousand people. Some might say it lacks the degree of sophistication the nickname indicates, yet Tromsø is a community devoted to fostering culture and education in a part of the world seemingly too physically demanding for cultural niceties to flourish. It is home to the most northerly, and the newest, of Norway's four universities, the others being in Oslo, Bergen, and Trondheim.

Most of Tromsø lies on an island, and two noteworthy features stand out at first glance. One is the bridge to the mainland, a span of thirty-four hundred feet supported by eighty-four pylons, which affords a clearance of 120 feet for ships passing beneath it. The other is Tromsdalen Church, an architectural gem often called the Arctic Cathedral because its dominant position, angular design, and frosty color bear striking resemblance to an iceberg.

North and east of Tromsø, the wooded, mountainous coast is modified, yielding to lower, but ever wilder, cliffs. Space seems to expand into a vast landscape as one rounds the top of Norway and nears the end of the *Hurtigrute* line—and the end of western Europe. Norway meets the Soviet Union at Grense Jacobselv, northeast of Kirkenes. The two countries share a 130-mile border, most of which is defined by the Pasvik River.

Sailing towards Kirkenes, ships reach the most northerly point of the route as they pass Nordkapp, or North Cape, which is considered the roof of Europe, although just next to it lies Knivskjellodden, not as spectacular but a mile farther north. However, it is to Nordkapp that visitors go. Here the sea crashes against a thousand-foot barren cliff. No trees adorn Nordkapp, only moss and scrubby grass, and in summer a few wild flowers. Gazing from that promontory out to the ocean, the traveler feels that this is truly land's end. Here at the edge of Europe, one may pick up a rock and add it to one of several cairns recalling other people, other journeys, and the almost cosmic emotions this sight has stirred through the centuries.

Yet Norway has land even farther north than Nordkapp. The archipelago of Svalbard — sixty-some islands overlaid with a blanket of eternal ice and snow many feet thick — lies midway between Norway and the North Pole. According to the provisions of a 1920 treaty, Norway governs Svalbard, but the forty-two signatory nations have equal access for peaceful commercial development. The several hundred residents who mine coal there for Norway and the Soviet Union share the space with seals, arctic foxes, and polar bears. Off to the west, some three hundred fifty miles north of Iceland, the tiny volcanic island of Jan Mayen is also part of Norway, but is inhabited only by arctic birds and foxes and a handful of military personnel monitoring weather and navigation.

These outposts are seldom visited by either Norwegians or other travelers. For most, it is sufficient to sense the lonely north at Nordkapp. Standing there in June or July, one can experience vividly the earth's summertime tilt that has given Norway the nickname, "Land of the Midnight Sun." Even in the country's most southerly areas, midsummer night is only a two- or three-hour twilight. In the north, night does not come at all. If the sky is clear along the northern coast, toward midnight one can

Moose near the Swedish border

At Akershus Castle in Oslo

watch the beguiling sight of the sun dipping slowly down and then beginning its rise again without ever touching the horizon.

Winter brings the reverse. At Nordkapp, there is no daylight at all for more than two months, and, even in the south, daytime lasts only about six hours. However, whether north or south, summer or winter, the weather is livable and activity continues. The combination of the arctic location and the warming Gulf Stream generates an incredible adaptation by all of nature, not least by human beings, who may live on very few hours of sleep per summer night, but make up for it in the winter. Occasionally in July, children are seen playing and parents gardening at two o'clock in the morning in the far north.

The drama of the seacoast is dazzling at every season of the year. But beyond its beauty, the presence of the sea exerts an influence on the entire country that cannot be overstated. Yet the seacoast is not all there is to Norway. Enchanting variety awaits the visitor going inland from any port. After sailing to the far north, it is a delight to return by auto to the south. Having seen the seacoast, the inland is easier to understand.

THE INLAND

The far north, Finnmark, is by all odds the least-known and least-visited part of the country, even by Norwegians, yet it has a haunting charm unlike any other area. It is mostly a plateau, called a *vidda*, bordered on the west by mountain ranges, on the south and east by rivers, and on the north by the seacoast, with its rocky promontories and white dolomite mountains. It is marked by scrubby birch and cottonwood trees, often twisted by the fierce winter winds, and a ground cover of springy moss and lichens. Low berry plants abound: bearberries (called in America *kinnikinnick)*, blueberries, and *tyttebær*, a type of wild cranberry known in America as lingonberry. Lakes dot the landscape, and the Tana River bordering Finland is one of the outstanding salmon rivers of Norway. Farther east, the Pasvik River at the Norwegian-Soviet border provides water power for residents on both of its shores.

On the *vidda* roam huge reindeer herds raised by nomadic *Saamis*, formerly known as Lapps. Reindeer endure the winter snow and cold, and feed on the *vidda* ground cover until early summer when they are driven to the seacoast for a change of diet, and for culling of the herd and butchering. If the timing is right, one can see hundreds of these hardy, majestic animals swimming to nearby islands for summer pasture. In late August, they return to the *vidda*. Some owners live out with the reindeer, as ancient custom dictated. Others have traded a nomadic lifestyle for homes in one of the inland *Saami* villages—Karasjok or Kautokeino — along with the majority of their fellow *Saamis*,

who are busy with other employment common to northern Norway. There are twenty thousand *Saamis* in Norway, and only 10 percent of them raise reindeer. Here and there along the northern highways is a round tent with several *Saamis* in their bright blue-and-red native garb, making themselves available to the tourist's camera.

Near Tromsø, as the long tail of Norway turns south, Sweden becomes its neighbor to the east, and the country narrows markedly. At Narvik, Sweden and the sea are separated by only four miles of Norwegian soil. Along this narrow strip which makes up one-third of Norway's length, there is but one highway, winding up and down the ever-present mountains, in and out of the narrow valleys. Sometimes one must take a ferry across the next channel or inlet; there is no bridge, no road around. Driving must be with careful deference to the unique conditions. With enchantment at every turn, the necessarily slower speed becomes a friend.

The visitor traveling south past Bodø—and a few miles farther crossing the Arctic Circle — is astonished at how far south one has traveled to reach what most would consider excessively far north. Along the way, the vegetation becomes more abundant. Evergreens — mostly pine and spruce — appear in some numbers, along with a greater variety of deciduous trees such as ash, alder, linden, and oak. Birds are plentiful, too: auks, puffins, cormorants, gulls, ptarmigan, and sometimes a white-tailed eagle wheeling overhead. Besides the reindeer, there are hare, elk, mink, moose, and even otter, who thrive in this land with its abundant waters.

Incredibly — in this terrain of mostly water, rocks, and nearly vertical land—there are also dwellings all the way, even villages and a few small cities. Most picturesque are the small homes of fisherfolk and farmers, perched in crannies barely able to accommodate them. It requires an adventuresome spirit or a lot of fortitude to manage this life, yet northern Norwegians—with a spirit similar to that of Americans in the open West—would not live anywhere else.

Skirting the Trondheim Fjord as one returns to the southern third of Norway, a more agricultural atmosphere pervades. Fields near Trondheim lie across mildly undulating terrain and look luxuriously spacious compared with farm plots elsewhere.

Trondheim is the northern gateway to the largest inland section of the country, an area of mountains, *viddas,* and rolling agricultural land. Although so much of Norway is near the sea, half of its area is more than one thousand feet above sea level, and one-fourth is more than two thousand feet in elevation. The proximity of the sea and the fact that at this latitude the timberline is approximately three thousand feet make even a seemingly modest mountain elevation truly impressive.

On the Sogne Fjord

The mountain ranges run generally from north to south, with the highest of them toward the west. Great, rolling plateaus are broken by thrusting peaks and long, deep valleys. Dovrefjell, the mountain area just south of Trondheim, is a non-glacial formation, which is one of the country's driest areas. Snøhetta, its highest peak at seventy-two hundred feet, keeps its majestic watch over the main north-south highway which bisects a wind-swept, barren plateau.

South and west of Dovrefjell lie the three great highland plateaus that give the southern third of Norway much of its special character. Toward the sea lies Jotunheimen, or "land of the giants," the largest massif in Europe north of the Alps. It boasts the highest peaks on the Scandinavian Peninsula, the king of which is Galdhøpiggen at 8,087 feet. Jotunheimen is a skier's and hiker's paradise and through the years has been the inspiration for folklore about giants and trolls inhabiting its far mountain reaches. On its seaward side, it drops through deep valleys aroar with cascades, on to the fjords and the sea — yet four to five feet of snow often remain along the roads, even in the summer. Near Trollstigveien — a spectacular, steep highway of switchbacks — it is quite common in June to see skiers negotiating the slopes in swimsuits.

Jostedalsbreen attains a height of seven thousand feet in some places and is the largest glacier in Europe. While this 340-square-mile ice field is the largest, it is simply one of many that dot the upper elevations, for glaciers make up 1 1/2 percent of the total land area of the country.

The Hardangervidda, a little farther south, averages only thirty-five-hundred-foot elevations. Above the tree line, it is a rolling, somewhat barren area where one may find the Three Billy Goats Gruff of the Norwegian fairy tales with their many cousins. The milk produced by goat herds yields the famous dark, nutty treat, *geitost,* or goat cheese. This open expanse gives way to numerous gentle valleys and crystalline lakes until it reaches the majestic Hardanger Fjord, whose inner tip is 110 miles from the sea and whose surroundings are abundant with fruit trees and breathtaking vistas.

Dotted on lonely heights and in secluded valleys are cabins, hostels, bed-and-breakfast homes, and tourist hotels — offering a wide choice of accommodations for those traveling between east and west. The roads, often precariously perched and amazingly constructed, pass through many tunnels, where the Norwegian highway engineers have worked seeming miracles through solid rock. Probably because of their greater experience, native drivers are more skillful than most visitors in negotiating the tight curves of these mountain highways. Frequent pull-offs allow for vehicles to pass where the roads are especially narrow. One pair of tourists in their small rental car met a tour bus coming around one of the typical, narrow curves. There was nothing for them to do but try to back up to the nearest pull-off. In the process, the rear right wheel went off the road, and the little car hung helplessly suspended. As the bus driver motioned the car's occupants to sit still, eight husky Norwegians jumped from the bus, lifted the little car back on the road, and directed it safely to the pull-off.

South of the Hardangervidda stretch the bleak heights of Haukelifjell, and the steeper, wooded slopes of Telemark, where the art of modern skiing was born. Beyond Telemark, the hills drop sharply into Setesdal — a valley so isolated it could be from another century — and then on to the sea.

There is scarcely a patch of level ground anywhere. Homes perch on the most precarious of slopes, and little fields demonstrate the most ingenious application of nearly vertical contour farming. Scattered bits of meadow are pasture to the flocks of sheep so common in this part of Norway.

Through its mountains flows one of Norway's greatest treasures, its "white coal." The seemingly unlimited supply of pure, rushing water tumbles from tarns and melting glaciers into thousands of waterfalls — to rivers and fjords below. Norwegian engineering skill has harnessed this tumultuous supply to provide hydroelectric power more than sufficient for the country's needs. Power stations are tucked into canyons, or even hidden inside mountains. As the water produces energy, it also surprises passersby with the cascading spray of a waterfall, the rollicking rush of a river, or the serene clarity of a lake sparkling in its frame of evergreen. Even an inlander is never far from water.

East of the mountain plateaus lies the most densely populated part of Norway. Foothills and valleys, thick with evergreens, are bisected by a maze of streams and dotted with lakes. In contrast to the cool, wet summers and relatively mild winters along the coast, here the weather contrasts are more extreme. Nesbyen in Hallingdal holds Norway's heat record of 97° Fahrenheit. With true inland extreme, its record low is minus 37° Fahrenheit.

Both summer and winter vacationers cherish these inland areas, since they are more quickly accessible for mountain sports than are the higher massifs. Cabins dot the landscape, reflecting rich opportunities for hiking, skiing, fishing, or hunting. In summer, Norwegians come here in search of the elusive and much-coveted wild *multer,* or cloudberries. Tradition says that if a patch of *multer* is found, one never tells where it is.

The more than 60 percent of Norway which is devoted to mountains and *viddas* makes way for fertile valleys, which broaden toward the border of Sweden on the east and the shores of the Skagerrak on the south. Yet despite these rolling vistas, only 3 percent of Norway is tillable, with another 25 percent being productive forest land.

An old ballad dance

Soccer, a favorite sport

Gudbrandsdal, the most famous of the agricultural valleys—and certainly one of the country's most beautiful areas — stretches 125 miles south from the skirts of Dovrefjell. The setting for Ibsen's *Peer Gynt,* it is not far from the high fastnesses suggesting the "hall of the mountain king," so vividly captured in Grieg's *Peer Gynt Suite.* Its lush farms and forests are the pride of its inhabitants.

At the south end of Gudbrandsdal lies Lake Mjøsa, a long finger of water stretching seventy miles and reaching a depth of 1,453 feet. Norway's largest lake, for years it has accommodated the steamers used for moving farm products toward their markets in Oslo and beyond. Like its sister lake, Rands Fjord, and others, it is sometimes called a fjord because of its long, narrow shape and its depth—although it is a freshwater lake.

In every open space between forests are grain and potato fields, pastures for dairy cattle, and plots yielding hay for winter fodder. Flowing through the timber and farmland of eastern Norway is the Glomma River, the longest in Scandinavia. It takes its rise near the old copper-mining town of Røros, provides power and transport for sawmills along its shores, and empties into the Skagerrak at Fredrikstad, east of the Oslo Fjord.

Extending northward from the Skagerrak for more than forty miles—to the city of Oslo at its inner end—the Oslo Fjord may be less dramatic than the west coast fjords, but it is the channel for ship traffic of every sort going to and from Oslo. It carries pleasure boats on short jaunts, as well as freighters and ferries headed out to the sea lanes that provide access to other world ports. Industrial developments, seeking abundant power and accessibility to transportation dot both sides of the Oslo Fjord. On its western shore is Tønsberg, Norway's oldest city, which was founded in Viking days.

Oslo, Norway's capital, is the nation's center for government, commerce, and cultural life. It is a city of one-half million inhabitants, with nearly that many more in contiguous communities. In the central city are the Palace, the Parliament building, and—on the brow of the fjord—Akershus castle, a historic old fortress. City Hall, a distinctive modern building facing the harbor, was begun before World War II and completed later. One of the many examples of Norway's legendary resistance movement during the Nazi occupation was the consistent frustrating of Nazi attempts to complete the construction.

Oslo is at once very modern and very old. New buildings, both completed and in progress, coexist charmingly with three- and four-story walkups on an intricate maze of streets. Visitors often remark on the cleanliness of the capital, as well as of virtually all of Norway. The natives tend to be good housekeepers even outdoors. They also blend a contemporary lifestyle with an active appreciation of their roots.

Oslo is the hub for both mountainous recreational paradises and bucolic homesteads. The railway system, with its ultramodern cars and reliable service, radiates out from the city on nearly three thousand miles of track, less than one quarter of which is on level ground. Norwegian trains pass through 775 tunnels and over three thousand bridges. Snow clearance, even in the most difficult settings, is superb. As Norwegians themselves say, "You can always go by train."

THE PEOPLE

Certainly, this is a country with all the ingredients to make an "international park." Yet despite the plethora of scenic riches, among the best of Norway's assets are its people. But what is it like to live at such a latitude? What if one works, raises children, and lives a lifetime in these extremes, rather than just enjoying the magnificent scenery as a visitor?

For one thing, Norwegians have plenty of elbow room. While there are only a few more than four million of them—less than the population of Wisconsin—they are distributed throughout the country in irregular fashion. Over three million of them live close to the sea; nearly the same number are town or city folk. The three northern counties of Finnmark, Troms, and Nordland compose one-third of the land area, but only one-tenth of the people live there. Mountains and valleys distribute people according to available land. In all of Europe, only Iceland has a lower population density. Daily living is often not easy, but toughness and resiliency are part of Norway's heritage and history—a past which bears pointedly on its life today.

Little is known about Norway before the eighth century, although recently discovered rock carvings and artifacts reveal details of organized coastal communities as long ago as the Bronze Age. In the ninth through the eleventh centuries, the isolation of Norway was broken and the attention of the western world was captured when the Vikings sailed forth to trade and plunder in Europe, or even, via river access, as far away as Constantinople. They established settlements in the British Isles, Iceland, and Greenland; Leif Eriksen led explorations as far as Newfoundland in the New World.

The Viking period contributed two great developments to Norway's history. First, after prolonged conflicts among local chieftains, the country was unified by Harald the Fairhaired. Second, Norway officially became a Christian nation under King Olav II Haraldsen, later canonized St. Olav, the patron saint of Norway. Subsequently, during the Reformation, the Lutheran Church became the official church of Norway.

The end of the Viking era brought a decline in Nordic identity abroad, and a loss of a third of the country's population by the

Say it with flags

Black Death. In the fifteenth century, Norway was absorbed by Denmark, and three centuries later—following the Napoleonic Wars—Denmark lost Norway to Sweden. Protesting its lack of self-determination, Norway called an assembly of elected delegates, which met in Eidsvoll; on May 17, 1814, the assembly adopted a new constitution. It was put into practice immediately, but, by mutual agreement, the Swedish king remained the monarch until 1905.

The period of Swedish rule also happened to be a period of economic hardship. Small farms, aggravated by serious crop failures, were not adequate to provide for a growing population. Many Norwegians left for America in search of better opportunities, particularly the chance to own land. Those who left rejoiced with the folks back home when, in 1905, Norway voted to become independent. The people elected as their king the Danish Prince Carl, who became the very popular King Haakon VII. From 1940 to 1945, Nazi Germany occupied Norway, so in modern times it has existed as a truly independent nation for less than a century.

As a constitutional monarchy, Norway is a democracy governed by the people through representatives elected to the *Storting*, or parliament. The chairman of the party in power is appointed as Prime Minister by the King, who exercises his influence through regular, frequent meetings with the ministers of government, and through his many ceremonial functions.

In 1987, King Olav V, son of King Haakon and Queen Maud, was feted for his thirty years as a beloved and democratic monarch. When he became King, he adopted as his own—and all through his reign has faithfully exemplified — his father's motto, *Alt for Norge*, which means "All for Norway." The royal family lives close to the people in spirit and in reality. Crown Prince Harald and Crown Princess Sonja assist King Olav in numerous domestic and international duties. The people regard their King with deep affection and appreciate his democratic spirit. They recount with pride his insistence that he wait his turn for medical attention like everyone else. They often tell how, during an energy shortage, he rode the streetcar to the ski runs at city's edge — paying his fare and fastening his own skis to the tram racks—just as is expected of any other passenger.

Norwegian life-style is a fascinating combination of juxtapositions — old and new, isolated and integrated, provincial and cosmopolitan. These disparities are reflected in language usage, for example. The mountains and valleys have separated the nation into enclaves, with a multiplicity of dialects reflecting great differences in vocabulary, structure, pronunciation, and even in the lilting "tune" with which some of them seem to be half sung. Total strangers can be quickly associated with a specific locale by their speech.

Dialects bear traces of the Old Norse of medieval times, as well as of the Danish that was the official language for so many years. Two standardized forms of Norwegian—*Nynorsk*, or new Norwegian, and *Bokmål*, or "book voice" — are taught in the schools, yet unique, localized practices persist despite efforts at uniformity. Because of the many dialects, there is great variation, not only in pronunciation, but in the spelling of many words. For example, Knivskjellodden, near Nordkapp, is spelled in at least four different ways, all of which are correct and reflect their individual origins.

A story is told of two Norwegians having a conversation about their mutual friend Pedersen. The first comments that Pedersen is quite a linguist. The other asks, "Is that so? How many languages can he speak?" To which the first replies, "Seven, and six of them are Norwegian."

Prolonged isolation has also produced sharp differences in perception among Norwegians from diverse areas. For instance, eastern Norwegians, as well as Bergensers themselves, considered Bergen a place apart. Since Bergen was the leading port during the Hanseatic period, its primary points of contact remained with England and Holland until 1909, when the railway finally connected it by land with Oslo. Despite modern communication, old habits die hard. A young boy whose family moved from Oslo to Bergen asked his father, "Will we ever go back to Norway?"

Conversely, Norwegians everywhere are alike in many ways. They have a keenly honed love of family and home, are civilized and good-humored, and respect the views of others. They patronize their numerous bookstores regularly and rank first in the world in the number of books printed per capita. The claim is made that the average citizen reads three newspapers a day, but time spent listening to the state-sponsored radio and television is minuscule by American standards. Norwegians are avid followers of politics and world affairs, however, and the annual awarding of the Nobel Peace Prize in Oslo underscores their deep commitment to peace.

Along with a keen national pride, Norwegians at times convey an air of charming diffidence, perhaps because traditionally they have seen their country as a relatively small player on the world stage. However, today it has become an advanced and strategic part of Europe.

By reputation, Norwegians are reserved, stolid people, and it is true that they are generally thoughtful and a bit cautious. Yet their hospitality is renowned. Visitors—even strange American cousins — are heartily welcomed, and often the United States flag is flown to mark the occasion.

Norwegians tend to be in tune with nature and are physically strong from intimate dealings with it. Their dwellings, both rural

Face-painting in the park

Starting young

A meal on the Palace grounds

and urban, demonstrate that they are masters at building on impossible terrain with poor access. Most of the homes are made of wood and painted in rich umbers and reds, deep blues and cinnamon browns, as well as in sparkling white.

Home interiors exhibit the same love of color. They may be furnished with antique, hand-carved, and hand-painted primitive pieces. There may be standard continental furnishings or the sleek, contemporary furniture of teak, rosewood, pine, or birch for which Scandinavia is famous. Cherished paintings, heirlooms, and photographs of ancestors are often featured. Flowers are used whenever possible. There are eating accommodations both at traditional dining tables and at large coffee tables where light repasts are often served. Each bed is equipped with a *dyne,* the down comforter used by Norwegians the year round.

Countless guests have lauded Norwegian cooks and bakers, who have plied them with a tempting array of whipped cream cakes, tortes, cookies, and delightful small waffles served cold with jam as a special treat with coffee. Norwegian smorgasbords set new highs in variety, abundance, and artistic flair. For simpler occasions, *smørbrød,* or open-faced sandwiches, are miniature marvels of taste and beauty. A Norwegian cook wants to be sure the sight is enticed first.

Bountiful dairy products mean that there is never a shortage of wonderful cheeses, or of thick cream to pour on a bowl of delectable strawberries. The Norwegians' frugal nature accounts for their staggering selection of dried, cured, smoked, or marinated meats and fish. Yet fresh seafood and fish are always available, with salmon and shrimp perhaps the most popular. Pork, mutton, and reindeer are usually of higher quality than chicken and beef. An everyday favorite is *får-i-kål* — a slow-cooked dish of cabbage, mutton or lamb, and black peppercorns. Boiled potatoes are almost always served, no matter what the main dish may be.

Christmas dinner usually features spare ribs, or sometimes a specially roasted mutton called *pinnekjøtt.* The *lutefisk,* or lye-treated cod — so popular among the immigrants to the United States — is still a cherished Christmas Eve tradition among some families, especially in specific areas. It is generally considered an echo of earlier centuries, with their more limited diets and lack of refrigeration.

The constitution guarantees religious freedom, but nearly everyone belongs to the state church. Many churches built soon after the arrival of Christianity are still in use. Some are made of stone, with thick walls and slit windows, for they were originally fortresses as well as places of worship.

Of particular interest are the almost thirty stave churches that remain from the early Christian period. They are made of plank walls erected on supporting posts, or staves, and are masterfully decorated inside and out with wood carvings in intricate plant and animal designs, many inspired by ancient legends. Gaping dragon heads on the gables were intended to keep evil spirits away, and are reminders of early efforts to integrate pagan symbols into the new faith.

It is not only in the stave churches that folk arts are valued. In many rural and urban locations, folk museums preserve not only the homes and farm buildings of centuries past, but countless everyday objects elevated from the merely practical to the truly exquisite through the application of folk art. The objects on display are testimony of long winter nights spent creating beauty to be enjoyed in the present and then passed along to future generations.

Skillful hands carved intricate ornamentation on ladles, butter presses, chairs, chests, even tools. Often objects were decorated with *rosemaling,* or rose painting, a highly stylized type of floral pattern done in colors characteristic of specific localities. Many a trunk came to America with the immigrant's name and departure date elaborately worked in *rosemaling.*

In a folk art exhibit, there also may be a Hardanger fiddle, the highly ornamented eight-stringed violin used for generations to accompany folk dancing. Four strings for playing and four more beneath them for sympathetic vibration produce in the hands of a skilled fiddler a sound akin to that of a bagpipe.

More modern artists strove, for the most part successfully, to develop beyond the folk dimensions. Many — such as dramatist Henrik Ibsen, composer Edvard Grieg, and painter Edvard Munch — studied on the continent. However, the results of their cosmopolitan training are still infused with the strong spirit and folklore of the homeland.

Today, the ancient arts are still practiced by a few artists, who also teach them to a new generation. Examples of this heritage coexist with late twentieth-century creations in remarkable harmony. Abstract paintings and sculptures, clean-lined jewelry, and atonal music reflect, each in its own way, the kind of land that gave them birth.

Earning a living has always required ingenuity in the rigors of Norway. Fishing, agriculture, and shipbuilding — for so long leaders in Norway's economy — have been subject to many changes in recent years.

Fishing represents a shrinking percentage of the total economy, but is more sophisticated and far-reaching than before. Herring, cod, capelin, brisling, mackerel, shrimp, salmon, and trout are the chief products; 95 percent of the annual take is exported fresh, frozen, dried, canned, or otherwise processed. Norway is the world's leading exporter of salmon, most of which is now raised on fish farms.

As fresh as it comes

The only local agricultural products available in sufficient quantities for domestic needs are potatoes and dairy products, although barley, oats, wheat, vegetables, and fruit are also raised. Farmers also own extensive forest lands; modern equipment and the rivers on which to float logs to market enable them to provide raw materials for domestic use and export of paper, furniture, boats, and prefabricated homes.

Shipbuilding has declined, although Norway's boatyards produce about twenty-five thousand boats per year, half of them for export. However, Norway's "floating empire," its merchant marine, is among the world's largest and transports goods internationally. In recent years, Norway's cruise ship business has earned an enviable reputation as a leader in offering luxury tours all over the world.

Norway bans nuclear power, but makes exceptional use of its most abundant resource, water. While the hydroelectric stations scattered along waterways in the mountains provide all the nation's electric power, they use only half of the available water. This lavish supply of energy has enabled Norway also to be a leader in aluminum manufacturing and to become increasingly important in the electronics industry.

While production of nickel, iron, steel, and aluminum and their accompanying technologies are moderately important industries, Norway's most valuable mineral comes from the sea. Since 1971, offshore oil drilling—first near Stavanger and now farther north — has assumed a critical place in the nation's economy. The area of offshore development is three times the land size of Norway, and production is strictly controlled by the government. The oil and gas produced account for 2 percent of the world's total supply.

Besides energy and oil and the sub-specialties they spawn, the largest single segment of the gross national product is human services—a direct result of Norway's social welfare system. This concern for individual well-being stems directly from the people's compassionate nature and their years of hardship, but it presents a demand that is never fully met.

And what do Norwegians do when they are not wresting a living from this somewhat resistant land? Or is the struggle for livelihood all consuming?

Music and sports are enjoyed by Norwegians young and old, through clubs and activities affiliated with school or community. There are soccer clubs, tennis clubs, cycling clubs, ski clubs; there are choruses, orchestras, and bands. All enjoy a great investment of the time and energy of their members.

Throughout the year, weekends are sacrosanct for recreation, most of it outdoors. Norwegians love to hike and do so in all weather. In summer, people camp or spend time at the *hytte*, the mountain or seaside cabin that many a family is proud to claim.

People swim, cycle, canoe, fish, and sail every conceivable type of boat. Whenever the sun shines, they will be found turning their faces, like flowers, to the sun, soaking up its rays against the dark days they know will come.

In cold weather, figure and speed skating, as well as ice hockey, all claim devotees. But the most popular of all sports is skiing, called in the Norse sagas "the sport of kings," but today the sport of young and old, mighty and humble. People ski on the pristine expanses of mountain and field, or on man-made ski trails, two thousand of which are floodlit to extend trail time in the dark of winter. Natives say that on a nice Sunday afternoon in winter, three hundred thousand of Oslo's five hundred thousand residents will be out on the trails. Holmenkollen, a ski jump at the edge of Oslo, is used only for the annual World Cup ski jump competition and its preliminary practice jumps. The World Cup day in March takes on truly festive proportions and is sometimes called Norway's "second national day." In the summer, the base of the ski jump where the competitors land is flooded and used as a swimming pool. Bands and orchestras perform from a portable stage, making use of the available seating.

All Norwegians give special attention to holidays. Those of religious origin, particularly Christmas, Easter, Pentecost, Holy Week, and St. Hans Eve on June 23—when Midsummer Eve is celebrated — are family-oriented and include as many contiguous days as possible. Constitution Day (May 17) and, to a lesser extent, Labor Day (May 1) are occasions for parades and public festivities. Beyond all these, there is *fellesferie*, the general holiday, which for most falls in July. The government guarantees all Norwegians four weeks of vacation. Even dairy farmers can have the time; someone is provided to milk the cows.

Norwegians appreciate a balanced life in their land of seeming imbalance. They have learned from their heritage to work, and now also have the luxury of play, which they certainly never neglect. While their land has been a hard master, they have made it also a diverting companion. Its rigors are at the same time its fascination.

A traveler booking her tenth trip to Norway was chided by a friend, "Why do you keep returning to the same place? Is it all those relatives you've met?"

"Well, yes, they welcome me so warmly and always urge me to come again. But it's something more, something almost mysterious. It's the sense of vigor, the crisp mountain air, the scenic grandeur of the fjords, the spell of the summer night. I always long to experience them one more time."

True, Norway is not an international park, but those who visit there cannot escape its unusual magnetism. It invites all who seek beauty and admire achievement to enjoy them in the Land of the Midnight Sun.

Tromsø's Arctic Cathedral

Regatta on the Oslo Fjord

Although almost three-fourths of Norway is covered by forests and mountains, trees are less plentiful along rocky seacoasts. There, buildings are the chief enhancement of the land. In Kristiansund, a west coast port city, the buildings may be painted in vivid colors, as well as in white. Scattered along winding streets, they form an attractive and varied pattern, appealing to the eye by land, sea, or air.

Wild flowers splash color on meadow and roadside. Besides the bluish-purple of lupine growing in this upland field, there are the gold of dandelion and buttercup, the white of daisy and caraway, the rosy pink of clover and wild rose, and the pink-to-purple of fireweed. More than two thousand types of flowering plants grow in Norway.

Trollstigveien, "the troll's ladder," approaches Romsdals Fjord from the south on Highway 63. Finished in 1936, this awesome highway zigzags down the mountainside in eleven tight hairpin turns, offering both a challenge to the motorist and one of the most breathtaking mountain views in Norway. Stigfossen, "the ladder waterfall," drops more than five hundred feet and flows under the highway.

The name, "The Land of the Midnight Sun," applies in a special way to the area north of the Arctic Circle, where, for more than two months of the summer, the sun never sinks below the horizon. In contrast, the sun disappears completely between mid-November and mid-January. Then, electricity provides light for activities. Here at Alta, on the north coast, the sky is a blaze of gold at midnight.

People relax on the lawn of Eidsvollsplass, an open area in front of the Parliament building in Oslo. There are eleven political parties, of which six are currently represented in the Parliament, or *Storting*. No party has a majority; cooperation is necessary to prevail on key issues. Norwegian citizens, generally well-informed on local and international issues, are active in political affairs.

Before the era of the automobile, capital cities in Europe, including Oslo, had mounted police as a practical matter. They were exceptionally effective at crowd control and became a matter of pride and distinction for every city boasting them. Now most often used for processions and ceremonial functions, those mounted police still in existence continue to stir excitement whenever they appear.

Clockwise from upper left. ■ This interior at Krossbu in the Jotunheimen area, typical of many old homes finished with natural wood, has modern conveniences, but the furnishings preserve the flavor of the past. ■ At the folk museum on Bygdøy in Oslo, a young woman models a *bunad,* the traditional costume characteristic of a particular community. ■ A wood carver works by his window at Dale in Sunn Fjord.

In the fifteenth and sixteenth centuries, Dutch ships came to Grimstad and other south coast ports to buy timber. It was not long before south Norway developed its own proud fleet of sailing ships. Homes in the southland, once painted in bright colors, are now generally white, for in the late 1800s, zinc mining made possible the production of high-quality, reasonably priced white paint.

The ever-present boats lie at the ready at an Ålesund dock. Living where water offers a convenient mode of travel—sometimes the *only* access to other communities — Norwegians use boats like those in other countries use bicycles or cars. Small boats are usually propelled by outboard motors, although oars are always available. There are eight hundred thousand pleasure boats in Norway.

Norwegians build homes and villages in all sorts of terrain, but locations near the sea have been preferred since Viking times for ship building, fish processing, and the services supporting them. Ålesund, on the west coast, is built on three islands, giving it a picturesque and fanciful appearance. Vacationers are drawn here by the feeling that Ålesund is an enchanted city risen from the folk tales of the past.

Sheep graze calmly among the rocks of a mountain meadow at Nystølen north of Balestrand on the Sogne Fjord. More common in Norway than cattle, sheep provide both meat and wool. A favorite dish is *får-i-kål,* a slow-cooked combination of mutton, cabbage, and black peppercorns. The world-famous Norwegian sweaters, regional costumes, and traditional rugs and tapestries are all made of wool.

A street in Stavanger retains the flavor of the past. The cobblestone pavement remains; houses, showing various signs of age, crowd the narrow sidewalk. Modern lighting has been added, and today's traffic makes its way, even though two vehicles may find it difficult to pass. Many old thoroughfares, now designated as walking streets with limited vehicular traffic, are used for outdoor cafes and open-air shops.

Modern shops offer goods from around the world, as well as from Norway's own factories, farms, and homes. Glasmagasinet, in the heart of Oslo, features Norwegian-made glass and crystal, along with many other products. Boutiques offer clothing, cosmetics, jewelry, paper items, and specialty foods. Book stores abound in this highly literate land. Bakeshops offer a tempting variety of breads and cakes.

The wharf at Bergen is often occupied by modern ocean liners. In contrast, the area's buildings are of many periods, some dating back to the Middle Ages. Successive generations continued that early style, giving the harbor a quaint, storybook appearance. A museum preserves relics of the Hanseatic period and is a reminder of the cosmopolitan life which typified this part of Norway's west coast so long ago.

■*Above:* The annual World Cup ski jump competition at Holmenkollen on the edge of Oslo draws crowds. The tower is 183 feet high, and the jumpers attain speeds of up to fifty-two miles per hour on the slope. Holmenkollen is used only for the World Cup in mid-March. ■*Right:* Bergen resembles Seattle, its sister city. They have similar climates, and both are west coast ports.

The open-air market at Bergen's harbor is a favorite shopping place for flowers, which Norwegians consider a necessity of life. In Norway, it is customary to bring a hostess gift when invited to dinner, and flowers are often the choice. To express congratulations or compliments, flowers are presented to either men or women.

This pastoral scene at Grindheimsdal near the Hardanger Fjord illustrates the variety of Norway's terrain. Almost two-thirds of the country is mountains and moors. In addition to the many fjords, fresh-water lakes and rivers make up nearly 5 percent of the total area. Some of the glacial lakes — long, narrow, and fjordlike in appearance — are called fjords even though they are actually bodies of fresh water.

Near Kolbeinstveit, natural beauty surrounds a sod-roofed *hytte,* or cabin, and a *stabbur,* or elevated storehouse. Thousands of waterfalls bring fresh water from nearby mountains. Norway's densely forested areas are filled with conifers — mostly spruce and pine — and with deciduous trees such as aspen, ash, elm, linden and oak. In the far north, birch and willow are the most common.

A river bed at Rindal, southwest of Trondheim, typifies a basic characteristic of Norway's terrain. Solid rock lies near the surface in most parts of the country, and the vagaries of weather and glacial activity have broken surface rocks apart and strewn them everywhere. Despite these obstacles, Norwegians find ways to grow crops in small fields. The area around Rindal produces both grain and livestock.

An hour's drive north of Oslo, the valley of Hadeland provides sites for larger-than-average farms that produce small grain, potatoes, and hay. Large barns house dairy herds and store feed for cattle. By the law of primogeniture, titles to Norwegian farms are passed from one generation to the next. Formerly, the inheritor was the eldest son; today, it is the eldest child, whether son or daughter.

Folklore tells of mountain trolls who lure passersby into their lairs. *Nøkken*, the water troll, lives in deep lakes and waits to drag unsuspecting victims to his watery home. In the sound of a waterfall, *Fossegrim*, the musical wizard, is heard playing his violin. Elflike *Nisser* live in farm buildings. If they are given porridge on Christmas Eve, they will watch over the crops and the animals all year.

The Lofotens are linked to each other and to the mainland by boats and other services. An expectant mother, being ferried to Tromsø Hospital by army helicopter, gave birth to a baby boy with the copilot's assistance. The two pilots presented the baby with a silver mug engraved with his name, date of birth, latitude, longitude, and altitude.

Clockwise from upper left. ■ Europe's largest high-mountain plateau, Hardangervidda, is a mecca for skiers. In the nineteenth century, Sondre Norheim of Telemark, the "father of modern skiing," devised stiff heel bindings, making possible sharp turns and leading to the development of slalom skiing. ■ A skier lifts her face to the sun. ■ Cross-country skiing is a favorite of health-conscious Norwegians.

■ *Above:* From Briksdalsbreen at the edge of Norway's largest glacial field, a mountain stream flows toward Olden on an arm of the Nord Fjord. ■ *Right:* In summer, an out-of-doors breakfast includes the ever-present crusty bread, ready to be garnished with cold meats, fish, cheese, tomatoes, cucumbers, and preserves. Boiled eggs, fruit juice, milk, tea, and coffee complete the menu.

■ *Left:* A wooden sailboat on the Oslo Fjord follows the tradition of seamanship begun by Vikings over a thousand years ago. Three ships from that period are exhibited at the Viking Museum in Oslo. Since the Viking heyday, Norway's merchant fleet has grown until today it ranks fifth in the world. ■ *Above:* Dozens of small craft, mostly for fishing, lie anchored at Svolvær in the Lofotens.

Midsummer Eve is observed on June 23, the eve of the feast day of Saint John the Baptist. It marks the year's longest day, when southern Norway has only two hours of dusk at midnight and northern Norway no darkness at all. Boats are decked with birch boughs as symbols of life, and bonfires illuminate the landscape. With similar emphasis on light, flaming torches are placed on graves on Christmas Eve.

Stone carvings reveal settlements dating back to the Bronze and Iron ages. It is believed that these carvings at Alta on the north coast are from 2,000 to 4,000 B.C. They depict organized teamwork and the use of domesticated animals in a bear chase. Before their discovery, this area was part of a development plan, but is now protected as a historic site. The carvings are colored red for greater visibility.

■ *Above:* Children often use the simplest of equipment to catch fish. ■ *Right:* A boat rests quietly in a harbor at Hellesøy, northwest of Bergen. The fisherman's life is demanding, for the sea can rage and threaten. Skill and knowledge — which are cultivated from childhood — are necessary, yet the industry continues; Norway has twenty thousand registered fishing vessels.

Exhibitions of folk dances are popular. The traditional accompaniment was the Hardanger fiddle. This highly ornamented violin has four normal strings, plus four more beneath them to vibrate sympathetically. Many other forms of music are also cherished in Norway, and modern composers contribute to virtually all forms of musical development.

South of Narvik on a twenty-mile stretch of Norway's chief north-south route, there are ten tunnels—the longest extending more than a mile and a half. Well-lighted and efficiently maintained, they pass through solid rock at the edge of the fjord to provide a twenty-foot-wide, two-lane road with numerous pull-offs for emergency use. Norway's highway engineers regularly meet challenges such as this.

It is hard to imagine that the quiet bay at Bjerkvik, north of Narvik, was a scene of battle and destruction in World War II. Bjerkvik is aptly named: *bjerk* means birch, a common tree in the north, and *vik* means bay. Place names in Norway frequently describe a feature of the location, so several places in the country may bear the same name. Family surnames have often originated in the same way.

Norwegians — never far from rivers — use them creatively. Logs are floated to mill and market; power is harnessed to produce more electricity than the country needs. This ecology-minded nation has developed policies to protect its rivers from pollution, and to keep a balance between industrial use of water and the preservation of nature. Many power plants include pools for raising fish to replenish the rivers.

■ *Above:* At Gran in Hadeland stand the Sister Churches built in the twelfth century. Restored in 1960, Nikolai Church is used for worship; Maria Church is open only for tours. ■ *Right:* Hillside farms, such as this one in Gudbrandsdal near Ringebu, help Norway remain self-sufficient in dairy products, potatoes, and most vegetables, but a substantial part of its total food needs are imported.

■ *Left:* Named for their vertical support timbers, stave churches, such as the twelfth-century Hopperstad Church, reflect skills used in building Viking ships. *Clockwise from upper left above.* ■ Norway's largest stave church is at Heddal in Telemark. ■ Both nature figures and Christian symbols are on the Uvdal stave church. ■ An ornate lock decorates the twelfth-century Uvdal stave church in Buskerud.

Northwest of Haugesund on the Akra Fjord, Kyrping Campground has cabins for campers and offers boating, swimming, and fishing. Fourteen hundred campgrounds — accessible by car, boat, bicycle, or on foot — are found in Norway. From these camps, Norwegians hike through mountains and forests and also enjoy such hobbies as photography, berry picking, and collecting plants or rocks.

Fresh crayfish, one of the seafood delicacies for sale in the Bergen fish market, await the morning shoppers. Shrimp, lobster, and mussels, along with many kinds of fresh fish, are equally tempting. Fish are sold in open-air markets, in meat-and-fish stores, or in specialty shops such as one near the harbor in Honnigsvåg on the north coast, which offers its wares under the sign, *Fiskebutikk.*

King Olav V, in military attire, arrives at Dombås in Dovrefjell for a special ceremony dedicating memorials to those who fought and died at Dombås in World War II. Among the casualties was the first American serviceman to give his life in the defense of Norway. King Olav, deeply loved by the people, travels extensively throughout the country, and is always enthusiastically welcomed wherever he goes.

South of Bergen is the eye-catching Slettebakken Church. Since the Reformation, the Lutheran Church has been the dominant faith and in 1814 became the official religion. Its expenses, including cost of buildings and salaries of pastors and other staff members, are paid by the government. The constitution guarantees freedom of religion; however 95 percent of Norway's churches are still Lutheran.

At Dale in Sunn Fjord, a typical window complements the view outside. Lace curtains or edging are commonly used, providing a setting to display bright, flowering plants either in window sills or in outdoor flower boxes. Fond of richly colored accents in their home furnishings, Norwegians also try to position their homes to take advantage of the natural beauty that surrounds them.

Built two hundred years ago, Vinje Church in Telemark is a cross-shaped wooden structure surrounded by a well-kept cemetery. Particularly in rural areas, Norwegians like to have the graveyard next to the church and near where they live and work. Parish records of birth, baptism, confirmation, marriage, and death are considered official and are kept on file in government archives.

■ *Above:* On Highway E6 south of Bodø, a stone pyramid marks the Arctic Circle.
■ *Right:* The Lofoten Islands are a large archipelago off the west coast north of the Arctic Circle. A busy fishing port, Stamsund is a base for trawling vessels and the site of two of the Lofotens' largest fish processing plants. It is also a stop on the *Hurtigrute* steamer line between Bergen and Kirkenes.

Near Geilo, goats and sheep roam along a main highway that crosses Hallingdal and the Hardangervidda between Oslo and Bergen. Goat milk yields a specialty food item, *geitost,* or goat cheese, which is used on Norway's famous open-face sandwiches, as a part of the breakfast menu, and in the rich, dark sauce served with reindeer meat.

In the Lofotens, boats carry fishermen regularly out on the rough seas to ply their trade, but even boats are finally retired. This quiet place of rest at Vestpollen is just a short distance from the port town of Svolvær, bustling with boat traffic and fish processing plants — including the world's largest fish oil factory. It is also home to facilities for storage of petroleum and energy, and to an area technical school.

A light blanket of snow frosts the trees in a forest south of Trondheim, the quiet broken only by the rushing of the mountain stream. Development of natural resources is evaluated in terms of its impact on the environment. Norwegians cherish their wild areas and are determined to keep the forests safe and the water pure.

In 1971, Norway became an oil-producing nation; today, it produces approximately 2 percent of the world's supply. Standing one hundred miles offshore west of Ålesund, this rig is one of several operated by the government-owned company, Statoil. Platforms run by domestic or foreign companies provide facilities for drilling, storage, and power production, plus housing for two to three hundred workers.

Norway's streams have work to do on their headlong rumble to the sea, for water provides power for the production of electricity. Tubes, sometimes several miles long, have been built through the mountains to harness these torrents and make maximum use of their energy. The same water may pass through several power stations, multiplying its contribution to the country's energy sufficiency.

The only railway north of Bodø crosses this narrow part of Norway, bringing iron ore from a few miles away in Sweden to Narvik for shipment to world markets. Port facilities include a completely automated iron ore loading dock — the world's largest — with an annual capacity of twenty-eight million tons. John Steinbeck's novel, *The Moon Is Down,* is based on World War II resistance activity in Narvik.

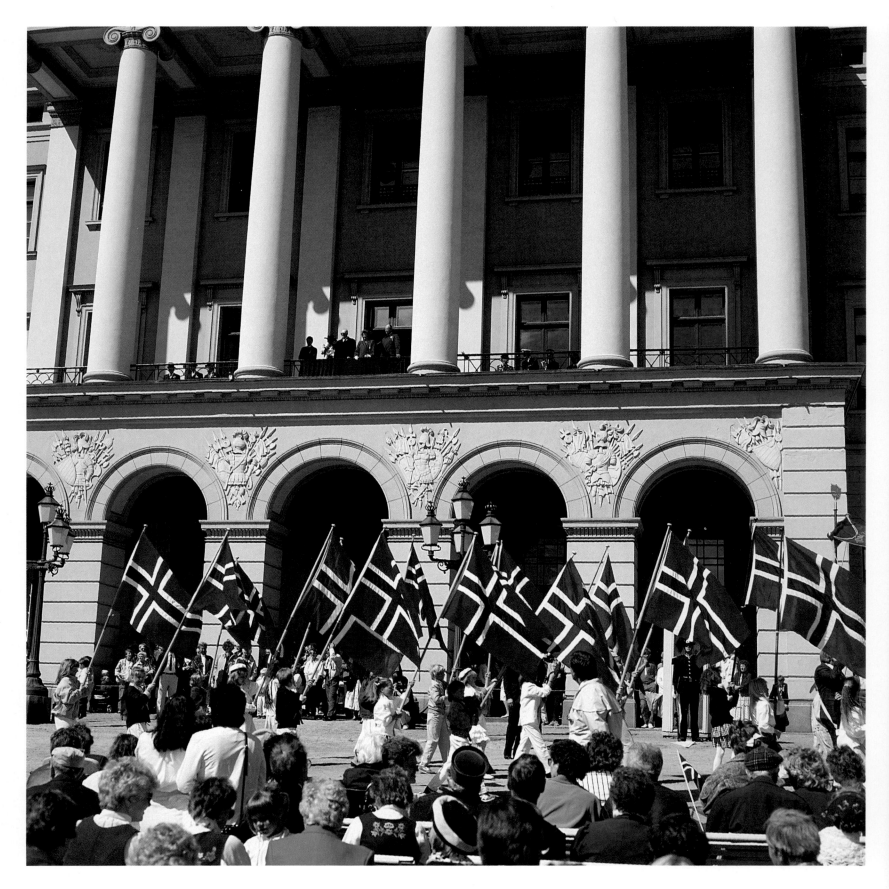

Syttende Mai, the seventeenth of May, is Norway's national day. In 1814, elected representatives met in Eidsvoll and adopted a constitution establishing a government for an independent Norway. Parades mark this day in many communities, with the most spectacular in Oslo. King Olav V, Crown Prince Harald, Crown Princess Sonja, Princess Märtha, and Prince Haakon return the greeting of the marchers.

Clockwise from upper left. ■ Secondary school graduates, or *Russ,* make colorful units in *Syttende Mai* parades. ■ Karl Johansgate—Oslo's main street—is always a popular place to stroll or shop and is filled to overflowing on *Syttende Mai* as the parade moves toward the Palace at its upper end. ■ Norway shares a basic flag design—a cross on a solid background—with Denmark, Finland, Iceland, and Sweden.

Off the north coast, in the Norwegian and Barents seas, commercial fishing is a major industry. Here the fishing grounds of Norway and the Soviet Union meet, and the two governments continue conversations about fishing rights. Much of the catch is dried on large racks like these near Alta. When dry, the fish may be sold whole or processed into fish meal. Rivers in Finnmark also provide sports fishing for salmon.

Having run aground and punched a hole in its hull, a fishing boat checks into a boat yard in Kristiansund. Twenty-five thousand boats are manufactured each year in approximately one hundred shipyards. Half of the vessels are exported; the remainder are added to the already vast number of large and small craft that work and play — and occasionally need repair — as they ply Norwegian waters.

■ *Above:* Employees adjust controls in a fish farm pond on the Sogne Fjord near Fardal. ■ *Right:* A fish farm shares the Nord Fjord near Stryn with passing traffic. Fish farming is a relatively new addition to the commercial fishing industry. Formerly, the fish were taken from the sea with nets, or caught in rivers and streams with hook and line.

■ *Left:* At Svolvær in the Lofotens, fish nets are dried and stored between expeditions for cod. ■ *Above:* Although modern tractors are common, a farmer near Florø on the west coast plows his plot using a fjord horse. In adapting to the landscape, this breed has developed broad musculature, short legs, and surefootedness — to cope with the most contrary, rock-strewn, up-and-down terrain anywhere.

■*Above:* Dots of gold reflect the springtime sun. ■*Right:* Farming takes on an added dimension when it is carried on in an idyllic mountain setting. In the midst of this beauty, the regular chores must be done. Here, hay is gathered from a small strip of land. Near a road known as the Eagle's Way, this farm above the Geiranger Fjord is one of the most photographed in Norway.

Gudbrandsdal, considered the "valley of valleys," stretches south from Dovrefjell for 125 miles. The highway winds along gently sloping mountainsides and broad expanses of fertile valley, past large farms that still bear names given many centuries ago. From Ringebu, in the center of the valley, one can see almost to those mysterious forests and glades where dramatist Henrik Ibsen set his famous story of Peer Gynt.

The pastoral beauty of sunsets in the midst of mountains, lakes, and fjords has always been wistfully cherished in the memories of the thousands of emigrants who have sought new opportunities in other lands, and is a normal part of life for present-day residents. Yet near this quiet, peaceful spot, the town of Førde is a center of industrial activity for the eastern part of the area known as Sunn Fjord.

In the fjord country, it is possible to travel only by some combination of land and water transportation, resulting in an average speed sometimes as slow as eleven miles per hour. While this pleases most tourists, it frustrates Norwegians. However, Norway is studying the idea of using huge pipelines, or "tube bridges," suspended in the fjords to speed north-south coastal traffic between Stavanger and Kristiansund.

From the village of Skei, south of Stryn, the edge of Norway's mightiest glacier is visible. Jostedalsbreen covers three hundred forty square miles, reaching elevations of more than seven thousand feet. Numerous smaller glaciers are scattered along its perimeter. Replenished by generous winter snowfall, all of them are huge water storehouses, constantly feeding the waterfalls, streams, and rivers below.

On Highway E68 northeast of Bergen, auto traffic follows a route marked by hairpin turns, dropping about twelve hundred feet in the six miles from Stalheim Hotel to Gudvangen on the fjord. Here, the traffic boards a ferry that sails along the Sogne Fjord, a sixty-mile water interruption on one of Norway's busiest east-west highways. At Lærdal, travelers resume the trip to Oslo by land.

Northern light lends an air of mystery to Bjerkvik beyond the Arctic Circle. North Norway's scenery has drawn generations of artists seeking to express not only its visual but its emotional impact. In fact, many Norwegians know this region only through painters, photographers, and writers. Fifty journalists recently traveled to north Norway on a program to acquaint them with its life and beauty.

Finnmark, Norway's most northerly, largest, and least-populated county, is home to twenty thousand *Saamis,* formerly called Lapps. Of these, only 10 percent herd reindeer, grazing their animals on the Finnmarksvidda and herding them by snowmobile in winter. Reindeer meat is popular in Norwegian restaurants. The *Saamis* also make use of the milk, hides, bones, and antlers.

Clockwise from upper left. ■ State-operated ferries are indispensable—linking islands to the mainland and to each other, joining highways across fjords, and providing access to nearby countries. ■ An accomplished wood carver, one of many noted for skill and creativity, works at his trade at Gran in Hadeland. ■ A man and woman do their chores in their dairy barn south of Trondheim.

Sima Power Plant was built half a mile inside a mountain on an arm of the Hardanger Fjord. Its annual output could supply power for a city of two hundred thousand for a year and a half. Norway's generators produce power both for domestic use and for export. But it is expensive power, requiring tubes running for many miles through mountains, and high voltage cables laid and maintained in rough terrain.

Even in modern Norway, many handcrafts survive. Here a master craftsman, eighty-five years old, shaves willow bough strips to be used as ties for handmade barrels. Artisans work with wood, glass, fur, gold, and silver. Wool is used extensively in knitting, weaving, and decorative needlework. The products of these crafts are sold throughout the country in cottage industry shops called *Husfliden*.

At the folk museum at Bygdøy in Oslo, dancers wear *bunads*, or national costumes, from various areas. Design, color, and ornamentation signify the locale. The intricately worked brooches (or *sølje*), buttons, clasps, and belts are of silver, gold, or pewter. *Bunads*, still worn at weddings, baptisms, national days, and other festive occasions, have been standardized only in the past century.

A common Christmas custom is the hanging of a sheaf of grain, or *Julenek,* to feed the birds. Following worship on Christmas Eve afternoon, church bells ring across the land at five o'clock. A family dinner and opening of gifts follow. The Christmas tree, aglow with white lights, is often placed in the center of the room so the family can join hands and dance around it as they sing Christmas songs.

The gracious interior of a home in Hadeland, north of Oslo, illustrates the Norwegian love of wood. Here the glowing, natural pine on walls, floor, and ceiling is a perfect foil for furnishings shaped directly from the nearby forest. Norwegian-made furniture, whether rustic or sophisticated, whether handcrafted or machine manufactured, is noted for the timeless simplicity of its function and design.

Home builders in Norway have always had to adapt to construction sites on other than level ground. Cities, faced with increased housing demands and limited space, now permit some development of apartment blocks massed on hillsides. One of these, at Bodø, north of the Arctic Circle, uses the varied colors popular for Norwegian homes and provides balconies overlooking the city and the sea.

■ *Above:* Many old buildings are now pre-served and exhibited in natural settings in folk museums. ■ *Right:* South of the Stor Fjord in Drotninghaug, farms enjoy a peaceful splendor, but farmers find it hard to live on beauty alone. Many must work part-time at fishing, timber-cutting, and other jobs. Government subsidies also sup-plement farm income, enabling farmers to remain on the land they have inherited.

Gol, Ål, and Geilo in the picturesque mountain area between Oslo and Bergen attract hikers, campers, skiers, and fishing enthusiasts. Between Ål and Geilo stretches the long, narrow lake, Strande Fjord. The eye-catching sight on its shore is sedge, a rushlike plant that grows in hummocks in wet areas. The acidic soil which encourages the growth of sedge is found in places where there is an abundance of conifers.

North Cape is *Nordkapp* to the Norwegians. Its Gibralter-like profile is one of Norway's trademarks. It is a thousand-foot-high treeless cliff jutting out into the Norwegian Sea at the north tip of Europe. *Nordkapp* has sixty-seven days of perpetual darkness in winter, and seventy-seven days of continuous daylight in summer. It is a favorite spot on the itinerary of travelers who hope to see the Midnight Sun.

Crossing the road near Lakselv in Finnmark, a reindeer herd heads for
the sea where the animals will swim to nearby islands to graze. Fresh
grass is a change of pace from the moss and lichen of the winter diet.
Before the reindeer return to the *vidda* in the fall, their *Saami* owners
will cut the herd and butcher the animals that are ready for market.

Norway's cruise lines, as well as those from other countries, ply the west coast, usually passing Lavik on the Sogne Fjord. Several of the Norwegian lines also offer tours to the Mediterranean, the Caribbean, and around the world. The *Sovereign of the Seas*, which was recently launched by its Norwegian owners, is the largest cruise ship afloat, with a capacity of twenty-six hundred passengers.

The interior of Oslo's City Hall is decorated with murals and tapestries depicting Norway's history and folklore. During Norway's occupation, the Nazis tried to complete construction on the hall which was begun before World War II. But, as Norwegians like to say, "Every time a Nazi brought three bricks in the front door, a Norwegian carried five out the back." Somehow, the building was not completed until after the war.

Artisans at Juhls in Kautokeino create and repair *Saami* jewelry in addition to fashioning unique contemporary pieces. Norwegian craftsmen use a variety of materials — silver, gold, pewter, and bronze — to produce both abstract and traditional jewelry, including accessories for native costumes and silver items enameled in vivid colors.

Norway Design in Oslo specializes in domestically designed and fashioned objects for the home as well as gift items. The country's glassworks produce conventional patterns, but also enable designers to create individually designed pieces. The best-known contemporary glass artist in Norway is Benny Motzfeldt, whose innovative treatment of glass has brought her critical acclaim in many countries.

Clockwise from upper left. ■ Fish for sale! ■ Hadeland Glassworks, in Jevnaker north of Oslo, has produced glass since 1762, first bottles, then household glass and lead crystal, and—in recent years—art glass. ■ *Rosemaling,* a type of floral painting developed more than two centuries ago, is used to decorate wooden utensils, furniture, and walls.

Since more than one-fifth of Norway is forestland, timber is abundant, and many towns have sawmills. In Hadeland, one such town is Gran, which means "spruce." Felling and foresting are controlled; at this latitude it takes sixty years for an evergreen to mature. Rivers transport logs, which become paper, furniture, prefabricated cabins, or skis.

Ardent fishermen in many parts of the world go about their business regardless of the weather. While most of the fishing done in Norway takes place in open water, ice fishing, a more sedentary sport, is enjoyed by some. Its success depends on the fisherman's patience and the lucky confluence of the fish's path with the solitary hole in the ice.

Norwegians are health conscious and stress good habits of diet and exercise. Believing in an active outdoor life, they spend much time hiking, biking, sailing, swimming, skiing, and in a variety of team sports. They sunbathe when they can, sometimes meriting the nickname "sun worshipers." Their concern for health expresses itself also in a government program that provides basic medical care for all persons.

One of Norway's best-known open-air markets is Bergen's *Torget*, or market square, which is a crossroads located at the wharf's edge in the center of the city. Here, it is customary to shop in the morning for the day's needs. By late afternoon, the stalls and produce have disappeared, the area has been cleaned, and the square is available for strolling, visiting, concerts, and other activities.

In Oslo's Frogner Park, more than two hundred human figures carved in stone or cast in metal by sculptor Gustav Vigeland portray human life from birth to death. This massive project was underwritten by the city. Norwegian communities frequently commission artists to create statues, paintings, murals, and other works of art for public places.

The Henie-Onstad Art Center at Høvikodden near Oslo is a museum of modern art donated by the famous figure skater, Sonja Henie, and her husband, Niels Onstad. The museum also houses her trophies and prizes. At age ten, she was the Norwegian figure skating champion, and went on to become world champion in ten successive years. She won the Olympic gold medal in 1928, 1932, and 1936.

■*Above:* The Lyngenalps are near Tromsø.
■*Right:* It was not always easy to drive through the area near Trollstigveien. Snorre Sturlason, the thirteenth-century historian, tells that eleventh-century King Olav II Haraldsen, Norway's patron saint, cleared the way through these mountains. The King so inspired his 400 men and 100 area farmers that "twenty men cleared stones that one hundred could not clear before."

Decorated with *rosemaling,* a corner cupboard in the Horg Folk
Museum near Trondheim was used for household storage. Situated at
the mouth of the river Nid and on the shore of a broad fjord, Trondheim
was the seat of early kings and a busy trading post. It is the site of
Nidaros Cathedral and a center for culture, education, and commerce.

At 63° north latitude, the blossoms of spring promise a rich harvest at Boggestranda. Apples grow this far north because a warm stream flows from the Gulf of Mexico to moderate Norway's coastal climate. The inland produces fruit also. Particularly popular are the exceptional strawberries. *Multer,* or cloudberries, which grow wild in the mountains, are an expensive and much-coveted delicacy.

Homes for the aging have traditionally been built in both rural and urban settings. This *aldersheim,* or old people's home, on the shore of Lake Mjøsa, illustrates the effort made to keep these surroundings as homelike as possible. As is the case in all medically sophisticated nations, Norway faces the challenge of providing the best environment for those whose life expectancy is increasing.

Blokktind, meaning "block peak," located a few miles north of the Arctic Circle, lives up to its name. While mountains in Norway do not compete in altitude with the Alps or the Rockies, their location causes them to share characteristics with those of greater elevation. Peaks rise from sea level, and because of their northern latitude, the tree line is very low. Many of them are snow-crowned all year.

Norwegian sweaters featuring intricate designs and rich colors are produced by hand and machine. They wear like iron and are comfortable for everything from skiing to quiet pastimes such as reading. It is said that the average citizen reads three daily newspapers. More books are published per capita in Norway than in any other country, and fifteen hundred libraries are scattered throughout the nation.